COMPLETE GUIDE TO GEODUCK FARMING

Comprehensive Techniques, Profitable Strategies, Sustainability Practices, And Market Insights For Successful Cultivation And Business Development

GIOVANNI MALAKAI

© [2024] [Giovanni Malakai]. All rights reserved.

Except for brief quotations included in critical reviews and certain other noncommercial uses allowed by copyright law, no part of this publication may be reproduced, distributed, or transmitted in any form or by any means, including photocopying, recording, or other electronic or mechanical methods, without the publisher's prior written permission. Write to the publisher at the address below, addressing your letter to the "Attention: Permissions Coordinator," requesting permission.

DISCLAIMER

This book's content is solely intended for informational and educational purposes. The author and publisher of this book make no express or implied representations or warranties of any kind regarding the completeness, accuracy, reliability, suitability, or availability of the information, products, services, or related graphics contained in it, even though every effort has been made to ensure their accuracy and dependability. You consequently absolutely assume all risk associated with any reliance you may have on such material.

The author's own experiences and studies serve as the foundation for the techniques and procedures covered in this book. They might not be appropriate for every circumstance or person. Before putting any advice or recommendations from this book into practice, readers should use their own discretion and take into account their unique situation. Consulting with qualified professionals who specialize in veterinary care and animal management is always a good idea. Any direct, indirect, incidental or consequential damages resulting from using or relying on the material in this book are disclaimed by the author and publisher. Any decisions made by the reader based on the information presented herein are at their own risk.

TABLE OF CONTENTS

CHAPTER ONE 13
  INTRODUCTION TO GEODUCK FARMING 13
    CHOOSING THE IDEAL SITE FOR YOUR FARM 13
    SELECTING THE RIGHT SWINE BREEDS FOR YOUR OBJECTIVES 15
    PUTTING UP APPROPRIATE FACILITIES AND HOUSING 16
    PURCHASING TOP-NOTCH BREEDING STOCK 18
    COMPREHENDING FEEDING PRACTICES AND NUTRITION FOR 20

CHAPTER TWO 23
  CHOOSING AND SETTING UP THE SITE 23
    STANDARDS FOR CHOOSING AN APPROPRIATE LOCATION 23
    EVALUATING THE SUBSTRATE AND WATER QUALITY 24
    GETTING THE FARM AREA READY 26
    REGULATION AND ZONING CONSIDERATIONS 27
    IMPACT ON THE ENVIRONMENT AND MITIGATION 28

CHAPTER THREE 31
  PURCHASING AND TAKING CARE OF SEEDLINGS 31
    WHERE TO GET GEODUCK SEEDLINGS? 31
    TAKING CARE OF AND MOVING SEEDLINGS 32
    SEEDLINGS' ADJUSTMENT TO THE FARM ENVIRONMENT 34
    FIRST PLANTING METHODS 35
    KEEPING SURVIVAL RATES HIGH 37

CHAPTER FOUR 39
  PLANTING METHODS 39
    WHEN TO PLANT: IDEAL SEASONS 39

  CONSIDERATIONS FOR DEPTH AND SPACING 40

  USING TUBES AND PROTECTIVE NETTING 42

  METHODS TO CUT DOWN ON PREDATION 43

  KEEPING AN EYE ON AND MODIFYING PLANTING TACTICS 44

CHAPTER FIVE...47

 FARM ADMINISTRATION AND UPKEEP 47

  TASKS FOR SEASONAL AND DAILY MAINTENANCE 47

  MONITORING AND CONTROLLING WATER QUALITY 49

  CONTROL OF PREDATORS AND INSECTS 50

  CONTROLLING GEODUCKS' GROWTH AND HEALTH 52

  MAINTAINING DOCUMENTS AND MANAGING DATA 53

CHAPTER SIX...55

 METHODS OF HARVESTING 55

  CHOOSING THE APPROPRIATE TIME TO HARVEST 55

  HARVESTING IMPLEMENTS AND MACHINERY 56

  METHODICAL HARVESTING PROCEDURE 58

  AFTER-HARVEST MANAGEMENT AND PRESERVATION 59

  MEASURES OF QUALITY CONTROL 61

CHAPTER SEVEN 63

 COMPILING AND STOWING 63

  METHODS FOR CLEANING AND PROCESSING 63

  PACKAGING OPTIONS AND REQUIREMENTS 64

  ENSURING THE QUALITY AND FRESHNESS OF PRODUCTS 66

  CONSIDERATIONS FOR LABELING AND BRANDING 67

  GETTING READY FOR MARKET DISTRIBUTION 69

CHAPTER EIGHT 71
STRATEGIES FOR MARKETING AND SALES 71
FINDING THE RIGHT TARGET MARKETS 71
FORMULATING A MARKETING STRATEGY 72
ESTABLISHING A NAME AND CREDIBILITY 74
DIRECT, WHOLESALE, AND INTERNET SALES CHANNELS 75
RELATIONSHIP MANAGEMENT AND CUSTOMER SERVICE 77

CHAPTER NINE 79
PLANNING AND FINANCIAL MANAGEMENT 79
FINANCIAL PLANNING AND BUDGETING 79
SOURCES OF FUNDING AND GRANTS 80
ANALYZING PROFITABILITY AND CONTROLLING COSTS 81
MAINTAINING FINANCIAL RECORDS 82
GETTING READY FOR AUDITS AND TAXES 83

CHAPTER TEN 85
FAQS & FREQUENTLY ASKED QUESTIONS 85
TROUBLESHOOTING TYPICAL PROBLEMS 85
FAQS REGARDING FARMING METHODS ON GEODUCK 86
MANAGING ENVIRONMENTAL DIFFICULTIES 88
ANSWERING REGULATORY INQUIRIES 89
EXTENDED SUSTAINABILITY MEASURES 90

ABOUT THE BOOK

For anyone looking to get into or advance their understanding of the geoduck aquaculture sector, the book "Complete Guide to Geoduck Farming" is a vital reference. The insightful opening of this extensive reference highlights the historical background and significance of the geoduck industry while offering a broad overview of the sector. It examines the main advantages and difficulties of geoduck farming, providing a comprehensive grasp of market demand and long-term opportunities for producers. This background information prepares readers to understand the subtleties of geoduck farming and its potential for sustainability and financial gain.

For geoduck farming to be effective, a suitable site must be chosen and prepared. The book explores the factors that should be considered while selecting a site, evaluating substrate and water quality, and making the necessary preparations for the agricultural area. In addition, it addresses zoning and regulatory issues, making sure local laws are followed, and stress the significance of minimizing environmental effects. These insights help farmers make well-informed decisions that improve their farms' sustainability and viability.

Purchasing and caring for seedlings is yet another important topic covered in the guide. It covers where to find geoduck seedlings, how to handle and transport them safely, and how to get them used to live on a farm. Farmers are equipped with the knowledge they need to start their farms successfully thanks to a detailed coverage of first planting procedures and strategies that guarantee excellent survival rates.

The guide also covers the best times to plant, how much space to plant, and how deep to plant to promote healthy geoduck growth. It emphasizes the use of protective tubes and netting, ways to lessen predation, and ways to keep an eye on and modify planting plans. Farmers may maximize production and efficiency by optimizing their planting procedures with the aid of these comprehensive guidelines.

Maintaining and managing farms effectively is essential for long-term prosperity. The book describes pest and predator control methods, water quality monitoring and management, and daily and seasonal maintenance duties. It also discusses how to maintain the health and growth of geoducks and stresses the value of careful data management and record-keeping. These procedures are necessary to keep a geoduck farm operating well.

In terms of harvesting, the guide offers a detailed analysis of when to harvest, what tools and equipment are needed, and a step-by-step procedure for harvesting. To guarantee product quality, post-harvest processing and storage procedures are also covered in detail. To sustain marketability and high standards, quality control procedures are prioritized.

The book covers cleaning and processing methods, packaging specifications, and ways to guarantee product freshness and quality. Processing and packaging are essential parts of geoduck farming.

It also discusses market distribution planning and labeling and branding issues, all of which are essential to building a trustworthy and prosperous company.

A thorough examination is conducted of marketing and sales techniques, encompassing the identification of target markets, creation of a marketing plan, and establishment of a brand and reputation.

The book covers a variety of sales channels, including Internet, wholesale, and direct sales, and it places a strong emphasis on the value of relationship building and customer service in boosting sales and client retention.

Planning and financial management are essential to geoduck farming's financial success. Budgeting, financial planning, grants, financing sources, cost containment, and profitability analysis are all covered in the guide. To assist farmers in managing their money efficiently and guaranteeing long-term sustainability, financial record-keeping and getting ready for taxes and audits are also covered.

The book answers frequently asked questions and concerns about geoduck farming. It offers solutions to commonly asked questions concerning farming methods, advice on how to troubleshoot typical problems and tactics for overcoming environmental obstacles. In addition, long-term sustainability strategies and regulatory issues are discussed, providing farmers with a thorough resource to properly manage the challenges of geoduck farming.

CHAPTER ONE

INTRODUCTION TO GEODUCK FARMING

CHOOSING THE IDEAL SITE FOR YOUR FARM

Selecting an ideal site for your geoduck farm is essential to its prosperity. Finding coastal locations with the right tidal range and water quality should be your first step, as geoducks prefer clear, nutrient-rich settings. Make sure the water meets the proper salinity and temperature requirements, which are usually met in areas with moderate weather.

Confirm the location's suitability by conducting comprehensive site assessments, which should include environmental impact studies and water testing. This helps prevent problems in the future that could harm the geoducks' health, like pollution or unfavorable weather.

When choosing a farm location, accessibility is yet another important consideration. It should be simple to access the location for routine upkeep, harvesting, and transportation.

Being close to suppliers and markets can lower expenses and increase the effectiveness of logistics. Assess the state of the infrastructure that is required, including ports, highways, and storage facilities. Take into account the laws and rules that control aquaculture in the selected region as well. To guarantee that the business is operating legally and sustainably, obtain all required permits, and abide by all applicable local, state, and federal requirements.

Lastly, a key factor in your farm's long-term sustainability is community integration and support. To establish trust and win their support, interact with local stakeholders such as residents, environmental organizations, and fishers.

Comprehending and resolving community problems can cultivate a cooperative atmosphere, which is crucial for the farm's longevity. An effective and lucrative geoduck farming endeavor can be established by carefully choosing the ideal site.

SELECTING THE RIGHT SWINE BREEDS FOR YOUR OBJECTIVES

Achieving your farming objectives requires choosing the right swine breeds. The qualities of meat, growth rate, and degree of adaptability to certain farming situations vary throughout breeds. Look at the breeds that can help you achieve your production goals, whether they are for breeding, fast growth for the market, or premium pork.

Popular breeds include the Duroc, prized for its robust health and rapid growth, and the Yorkshire, noted for its superior meat quality and maternal qualities.

While selecting breeds, take into account the farm's environmental factors. Certain pig breeds have greater resistance to specific climates and diseases. For example, the Landrace breed is ideal for intensive agricultural operations because of its capacity to reproduce prolifically and its tolerance to confinement, but the Berkshire breed thrives in milder temperatures and yields meat with marbling.

You may maximize animal health and output by choosing breeds that are compatible with your local climate and agricultural methods.

Finally, consider how easily accessible and available breeding stock is for the breeds you have selected. Build trusting connections with respectable farms and breeders to guarantee a steady supply of superior animals. Selecting animals from a variety of respectable breeders can help minimize inbreeding and improve the overall performance of your swine operation.

Genetic diversity is essential for preserving herd health and enhancing qualities over time. You may successfully achieve your production targets and guarantee the prosperity of your farm by selecting the right swine breeds with care.

PUTTING UP APPROPRIATE FACILITIES AND HOUSING

For your pigs to be healthy and productive, you must provide an ideal living environment.

First things first, make sure your enclosures and shelters have enough room, ventilation, and weather protection. Swine requires ample space to walk around, relax, and readily reach food and water.

To keep the temperature at a comfortable level and avoid respiratory ailments, proper ventilation is essential. Build with sturdy materials that are easy to clean and disinfect and can endure the demands of farm life.

Provide spaces for feeding, watering, and waste disposal in addition to the pens. For the health of pigs, clean, easily available water supplies are essential, and automated feeding systems can guarantee constant nutrition.

Install effective mechanisms for managing waste to handle manure and lower the danger of illness. Maintaining a clean atmosphere and limiting the growth of dangerous germs and parasites is made possible by following proper drainage and sanitation procedures.

To maintain the health of the animals and lower veterinary expenses, clean and disinfect the premises regularly.

In swine housing, safety and biosecurity precautions are equally crucial. Establish procedures to regulate the movement of humans and animals on the farm to stop the entry and spread of illnesses. To improve biosecurity, use footbaths, barriers, and sanitation stations.

The health of the herd must be regularly monitored and maintained through immunizations and health examinations. Establishing suitable accommodation and amenities fosters a secure and efficient atmosphere that upholds the general prosperity of your swine farming enterprise.

PURCHASING TOP-NOTCH BREEDING STOCK

To build a profitable swine farming business, investing in high-quality breeding stock is essential. Begin by obtaining animals from respectable breeders who have a history of raising pigs that are healthy and productive. Seek for animals that exhibit desirable qualities like growth rate, meat quality, and reproductive efficiency, together with strong genetics and physical health. Make sure the animals are healthy and free of infections and genetic flaws by doing comprehensive inspections and health checks.

Examine the animals you plan to buy's performance history and breeding history. Weaning weight, growth rate, and litter size data can all provide important clues about the genetic potential of the breeding stock. Select animals with decent temperaments and strong maternal instincts; these qualities will have a big influence on your herd's management and productivity. Take into account whether the breeding stock is compatible with the unique conditions and management techniques of your farm.

After obtaining the breeding stock, put in place a thorough nutritional and health program to enhance their overall health and reproductive efficiency.

A healthy diet catered to their requirements should be given, and frequent veterinary care—including immunizations and parasite control—should be guaranteed. Keep meticulous records of their breeding cycles, pregnancies, and offspring performance, and keep a constant eye on their health. You may create a strong and profitable swine farming business by properly obtaining and managing high-quality breeding stock.

COMPREHENDING FEEDING PRACTICES AND NUTRITION FOR SWINE

For pigs to develop, stay healthy, and be productive, they need to be fed properly. Create a well-rounded diet that satisfies the dietary needs of growing animals at varying stages of development, ranging from piglets to adult breeding stock. Vital elements including proteins, carbs, fats, vitamins, and minerals should all be included in the diet.

To guarantee ideal growth and development, premium feed ingredients are needed, including grains, soybean meal, and vitamins. Adjust the feeding schedule to your swine's requirements, taking into account things like age, weight, and desired yield.

Use effective feeding techniques to provide a steady and sufficient intake of nutrients. Reduce labor expenses and waste by using automated feeders and waterers to offer a consistent supply of feed and water. Observe the animals' feed intake and modify the feeding schedules by their body condition and growth rates.

Make sure the feed satisfies the requirements by testing it frequently for quality and nutrient content. Feed should be handled and stored carefully to avoid contamination and spoiling, which can be harmful to swine health.

Additionally, emphasis on avoiding and controlling dietary shortages and diseases. Together with an animal nutritionist or veterinarian, create a thorough feeding schedule that takes into account the unique requirements of your herd. Frequent health examinations and dietary evaluations might assist in detecting and resolving any problems quickly. Providing your pigs with a healthy, varied diet not only encourages development and productivity but also improves their general health and well-being, which is essential for a profitable farming enterprise.

CHAPTER TWO

CHOOSING AND SETTING UP THE SITE

STANDARDS FOR CHOOSING AN APPROPRIATE LOCATION

It's important to pick a location for geoduck farming that provides the ideal environmental conditions for the clams to flourish. Because geoducks must burrow deeply, the site should have a firm, soft substrate, such as mud or sand. Seek out areas where human activity and natural occurrences, such as storms or strong currents, are less likely to damage the clams' environment.

Another important factor is accessibility; there shouldn't be any major logistical obstacles in getting to the site for routine maintenance and monitoring.

Another crucial element is the tidal range. Because these areas offer access to nutrient-rich waters, geoducks are more attracted to shallow subtidal and intertidal zones.

Tidal flushing in these regions should be done regularly to keep the water quality high and avoid stagnation. Make sure the location is well-suited for the geoducks' growth and health, with a reasonable tidal range that protects them from extreme weather. Managing water drainage and access can also be aided by a site with a gradual slope.

Finally, take into account how close other farming or aquaculture enterprises are. While some closeness to other farms might promote resource sharing and community support, too close contact could result in resource competition or a higher risk of disease transmission. To guarantee that the chosen location provides the ideal circumstances for sustainable and fruitful geoduck farming, a balance must be established.

EVALUATING THE SUBSTRATE AND WATER QUALITY

An important factor in a geoduck farm's performance is the quality of the water. The water must be pure, devoid of impurities, and the proper salinity.

It is crucial to do routine testing for pollutants such as industrial pollutants, insecticides, and heavy metals. The appropriate temperature range for water is between 10°C and 18°C, while the ideal salinity is between 27 and 35 parts per thousand (ppt). The geoducks may become stressed and experience changes in growth and survival rates if these criteria are significantly deviated from.

The substrate in which geoducks burrow must be carefully inspected. Because big boulders and other debris might impede the geoducks' ability to burrow, they prefer sandy or muddy soils. To make sure the substrate has the right grain size and content, perform a sediment analysis. High levels of organic matter can be advantageous because they foster a diverse microbial population that provides food for geoducks.

The water body needs to be biologically assessed in addition to physically. Pathogenic bacteria and hazardous algal blooms can be monitored to stop outbreaks that could wipe out the farm.

To maintain ideal conditions for geoduck farming, a continuous management plan should include regular sampling and laboratory studies.

GETTING THE FARM AREA READY

To ensure a level and smooth substrate, site cleaning and leveling are the first steps in preparing the farming field. Get rid of any big rocks, trash, and plants that can prevent geoducks from burrowing. Depending on the site's size and condition, either manual tools or machines may be used in this operation. Maintaining a level surface facilitates uniform growth throughout the farming area and aids in the dispersal of seed clams.

After the area has been cleaned, putting up fences or netting can assist keep birds, crabs, and other marine animals from preying on the area. To keep these barriers functional, they need to be firmly fastened and inspected frequently. It is advised that biodegradable materials be used for these constructions to reduce their negative environmental effects.

Following the physical preparation, the farming plots must be properly marked and mapped. To facilitate methodical planting and observation, divide the space into manageable portions. Weather- and tide-resistant markers must be used to identify each plot. This organization helps to ensure effective farm management and maximize productivity by monitoring growth rates, health assessments, and harvesting schedules.

REGULATION AND ZONING CONSIDERATIONS

For geoduck farming to be legal and use sustainable practices, zoning, and regulatory standards must be followed. To start, find out which local, state, and federal agencies have the authority over aquaculture in your area by contacting them. Environmental impact studies, operational permissions, and site placement limitations are a few examples of these rules. Adherence to these regulations is crucial to avert legal issues and guarantee the farm's sustained profitability.

To get support for your farming project, interact with community stakeholders and municipal zoning boards.

To resolve any concerns raised by local people and environmental organizations, public hearings, and consultations might be necessary. Gaining community support and facilitating a more seamless project clearance process can be achieved by open communication regarding farming techniques, environmental protections, and economic rewards.

Furthermore, be mindful of any limitations about the preservation of delicate environments and threatened species. To lessen possible effects on the environment, regulatory organizations may enforce certain requirements. Make sure that the methods you use for farming are in line with these circumstances.

To reduce ecological disruptions and advance sustainability, consider implementing buffer zones and habitat restoration programs.

IMPACT ON THE ENVIRONMENT AND MITIGATION

Sustainable operations depend on an understanding of and mitigation of the environmental impact of geoduck farming. To begin with, carry out a comprehensive environmental impact assessment (EIA) to determine any possible threats to the nearby ecology. Water quality, sediment disturbance, and the impact on the local flora and wildlife should all be included in this assessment. Consulting with environmental specialists can yield insightful advice and suggestions for reducing adverse effects.

Putting best management practices (BMPs) into action is essential to lessening the environmental impact of the farm. These methods include keeping a close eye on the quality of the water, regulating nutrient supplies to avoid eutrophication, and limiting sediment flow. Using methods like reseeding and rotational harvesting can assist preserve the ecological balance and guarantee the farming area's long-term health.

Implement conservation strategies in your agricultural endeavors. Within the farming area, protected zones can be established to encourage the recovery of overexploited species and maintain biodiversity.

Review and revise your environmental management strategy regularly to account for evolving circumstances and new scientific discoveries. Setting environmental stewardship as a top priority will help you make sure your geoduck farm benefits the neighborhood ecology and community.

CHAPTER THREE

PURCHASING AND TAKING CARE OF SEEDLINGS

WHERE TO GET GEODUCK SEEDLINGS?

It's essential to start your geoduck farming endeavor with high-quality seedlings. The main places to find geoduck seedlings are marine aquaculture-focused nurseries and hatcheries. Reputable hatcheries maintain the genetic health and viability of their seedlings by adhering to strict regulations. Give preference to sources who have a track record of producing healthy, disease-free seedlings. Making connections with regional aquaculture associations can also assist you in locating reliable vendors and learning about their processes for producing seedlings.

Buying directly from hatcheries frequently has the advantage of bringing you in contact with specialists who may provide insightful guidance on handling and planting.

The age and size of the seedlings are usually provided in detail by these facilities, which is essential for organizing your planting timetable. Large-scale operations may benefit from the bulk savings or regular supply contracts that certain hatcheries provide. Always use references, site visits, or reviews to confirm the supplier's legitimacy.

As part of conservation or research activities, it's also possible to look into community-based programs or partnerships with research institutions that might offer seedlings at discounted prices or even for free. These initiatives may provide an affordable means of obtaining seedlings while promoting environmentally friendly aquaculture methods. Make certain that any seedlings acquired from these sources adhere to the same quality and health requirements as those originating from commercial hatcheries.

TAKING CARE OF AND MOVING SEEDLINGS

To maintain the survival and well-being of geoduck seedlings, careful handling and transportation are essential. To ensure ideal oxygen levels, seedlings are usually transported in aerated containers filled with seawater. Maintaining a consistent temperature throughout transportation, often between 5°C and 10°C, is crucial to reducing stress on the seedlings. This temperature control can be accomplished with coolers or insulated containers, particularly on longer trips.

Reducing the amount of time spent traveling is another important consideration. The danger of stress and mortality increases with the length of time the seedlings are in transit. To guarantee the fastest possible journey time from the hatchery to your farm, arrange your logistics. To avoid heat stress, try to work with the supplier to arrange pickup times during the cooler hours of the day. Furthermore, it is essential to handle the fragile seedlings gently when loading and unloading to prevent bodily harm.

As soon as you get to the farm, start acclimating the seedlings to the nearby ocean. To assist the seedlings adapt to the temperature, salinity, and other water quality criteria of their new habitat, this technique entails gradually blending the farm water and the transport water over a few hours. This slow acclimatization lessens shock and raises the likelihood of development and adaptation that will be successful.

SEEDLINGS' ADJUSTMENT TO THE FARM ENVIRONMENT

A crucial stage that calls for accuracy and patience is acclimating geoduck seedlings to their new surroundings. To progressively equalize temperatures, start by submerging the shipping containers in the farm's water. Gradually add little volumes of farm water to the containers over the next few hours, letting the seedlings become used to the variations in pH and salinity. Although it may take several hours, this procedure is crucial for lowering tension and avoiding shock.

Keep a close eye on the water quality metrics as you become acclimated. Check the temperature, salinity, pH, and oxygen content of the farm water as well as the shipping containers using a portable water quality meter. The water mixing ratio should be changed to account for any notable differences. Maintaining a record of these factors can facilitate an easier transition for the seedlings by allowing for the early detection of any possible problems.

Keep an eye out for any indications of stress in the seedlings during this acclimation stage, such as gaping shells or decreased activity. When placed in a farm environment, healthy geoduck seedlings should seem attentive and begin to burrow gradually.

Isolate any seedlings exhibiting ongoing stress indicators, and proceed with the acclimatization procedure more gradually. Establishing a tranquil and steady atmosphere during this preliminary phase lays the groundwork for prosperous expansion and advancement.

FIRST PLANTING METHODS

To increase their chances of survival and growth, geoduck seedlings must be planted in a precise location in their first planting. Choose a location with ideal circumstances, such as muddy or sandy substrates that allow geoducks to dig with ease. Additionally, the site needs sufficient water flow to guarantee a steady supply of oxygen and nutrients. Mark out the planting grid before you begin to plant to maintain uniform spacing and avoid overcrowding, which may cause competition for resources.

Make holes in the substrate with a planting tool, like a planting tube or dibble stick. With a tiny margin for growth, the holes should be deep enough to hold the entire seedling. Making sure the siphon—the portion of the geoduck that rises above the substrate—is facing upward, carefully plant the seedling into the hole. To help with feeding and breathing, loosely cover the seedling with the substrate, leaving the siphon exposed. The geoduck quickly establishes itself thanks to this deliberate positioning.

After planting, keep an eye on the area to make sure the conditions are still ideal and to look for any seedlings that may have come loose. To protect the seedlings from predators like crabs and sea stars, utilize protective netting or predator exclusion devices. For the seedlings to settle and start their growth cycle properly, regular observation and care are essential during the first few weeks.

KEEPING SURVIVAL RATES HIGH

A combination of vigilant observation, predator management, and preservation of ideal environmental conditions is needed to guarantee excellent survival rates for geoduck seedlings.

Keep an eye out for indications of predators in the planting area and take the necessary precautions to keep them away. This could involve utilizing repellents, erecting physical barriers, or capturing and removing predators.

Furthermore, keep an eye out for any compositional changes in the substrate that can have an impact on the seedlings' capacity to burrow and develop.

Another crucial component is maintaining the quality of the water. Monitoring temperature, salinity, pH, and dissolved oxygen levels regularly helps guarantee that the environment stays in the ideal range for geoduck growth. Take immediate corrective action if any parameters are found to be outside of the optimal range. Consider using aeration techniques, for instance, to increase water circulation and oxygenation if oxygen levels are low.

Providing the right nutrients to the geoduck farm can help increase survival rates. Growth can be accelerated by adding phytoplankton or carefully prepared meals to the natural food source, particularly in the early stages. Monitoring and documenting growth rates and health indicators regularly facilitates tracking the effectiveness of your agricultural methods. The survival and growth of your geoduck seedlings can be maximized by creating a conducive environment that combines responsive modifications with proactive maintenance.

CHAPTER FOUR

PLANTING METHODS

WHEN TO PLANT: IDEAL SEASONS

It is essential to know when to plant geoducks to maximize output and ensure effective growth. When water temperatures start to rise in late spring or early summer, it's the best time to plant geoducks since it creates an ideal environment for the clams to settle in. The warmer waters at this time of year increase the chances of juvenile geoducks surviving, enabling them to burrow well and start their growth cycle with less stress.

Planting within this window of opportunity also benefits from the natural rise in plankton, which is the main food source for geoducks. After planting, it is important to make sure the clams have plenty of food available since this promotes their quick development and habitat acclimation. To find the best time to plant, farmers should keep an eye on historical data and trends in the local water temperature. They should also modify their schedules slightly in response to annual climate variations.

You mustn't plant in late fall or early winter when the water is much colder. Geoduck metabolic rates can be slowed down by cold, which can result in increased mortality and poor growth performance. The newly planted geoducks may also be disturbed by the harsher weather and increased risk of storms during these months, which could lead to them becoming too deeply buried in the substrate or dislodged.

CONSIDERATIONS FOR DEPTH AND SPACING

In geoduck farming, proper spacing and depth are essential since they have a direct impact on growth rates and general health. It is suggested that you space your geoduck plants at least one foot apart. By keeping space apart, overcrowding is avoided, which can reduce competition for resources and food and eventually impede growth. Better water circulation surrounding each geoduck is made possible by adequate spacing, which also lowers the chance of disease transmission and guarantees that every clam has access to enough nutrients.

Equally crucial is the planting depth of geoducks. The ideal placement for geoducks is both shallow enough to enable them to extend their siphons into the water column for feeding and deep enough to shield them from surface predators.

Generally speaking, planting depths of 10 to 12 inches work well. This depth guarantees that the geoducks can reach the surface without using too much energy and are firmly embedded in the substrate.

The geoducks must be handled very gently when planting to protect their delicate siphons. Reaching the proper depth every time can be facilitated by using specialized planting equipment. To make sure the geoducks have not been disturbed and that the spacing is still appropriate as the clams grow, farmers should inspect the planting area regularly.

USING TUBES AND PROTECTIVE NETTING

To protect juvenile geoducks from predators and environmental stressors during their early stages of maturation, protective nets and tubes are essential. Usually put in place right away after planting, these defenses create a physical barrier that keeps off predators including fish, birds, and crabs.

Typically, the netting is composed of a robust, UV-resistant material that can tolerate harsh maritime conditions while yet permitting the passage of water and nutrients.

To keep predators from digging up individual geoducks, tubes are often erected around them. These tubes are composed of PVC or a related material. Additionally, by stabilizing the substrate surrounding the geoducks, these tubes facilitate their establishment and growth. To enable the siphon to extend organically, the tubes are placed into the substrate with the geoduck planted within, making sure that the top of the tube is level with the surface.

To guarantee the efficiency of the protective tubes and nets, regular maintenance is required. Debris may build up over time, or materials may move as a result of wave and current action. To guarantee continuous protection throughout the growth phase, farmers should inspect the protective measures regularly and replace or alter them as necessary.

METHODS TO CUT DOWN ON PREDATION

A major problem in geoduck farming is reducing predation because many kinds of marine creatures are drawn to these clams. Predator exclusion tools, such as mesh covers or planting beds resistant to predators, are one useful tactic. These barriers let nutrients and water through while keeping larger predators from reaching the geoducks. It is essential to regularly inspect and maintain these devices to make sure they continue to function properly.

Using natural repellents or deterrents is another tactic. Some farmers scare off birds and other predators with decoys or noise-making equipment.

Furthermore, the planting area can be treated with eco-friendly repellents to keep fish and crabs away from it. The repellents must be safe for both the geoducks and the surrounding habitat, which calls for cautious application and selection.

Reducing predation can also be aided by increasing habitat complexity. Farmers can hide places for geoducks and throw off predators' hunting routines by erecting artificial reefs or mounds of rocks around their land.

This method contributes to a healthy marine ecosystem by protecting the geoducks and fostering biodiversity in the farming region.

KEEPING AN EYE ON AND MODIFYING PLANTING TACTICS

For geoduck farming to be successful, farmers must continuously monitor the clams' growth and health to make the required modifications to planting plans. It is important to regularly evaluate the planting location to look for evidence of disease, predation, or environmental stress. Data on geoduck conditions and growth rates can be obtained by farmers through the use of underwater cameras, divers, or other monitoring techniques.

Farmers can modify planting tactics to maximize growth and survival rates by using the monitoring data. For example, more protective measures like strengthened netting or more predator exclusion devices may be required if predation is higher than anticipated. Farmers may need to reevaluate spacing and depth or think about supplemental feeding techniques to improve nutrient availability if growth rates fall short of expectations.

It is also essential to adjust to changes in the surroundings. Farmers who grow geoduck should keep up to date on local water quality conditions, temperature swings, and any contamination sources. Proactively modifying planting tactics in response to these variables can assist reduce risks and guarantee the farming operation's long-term viability. Maintaining current best practices in light of fresh findings and technological developments will also help geoduck farming become more successful and productive overall.

CHAPTER FIVE

FARM ADMINISTRATION AND UPKEEP

TASKS FOR SEASONAL AND DAILY MAINTENANCE

In geoduck farming, daily maintenance entails regular inspections and actions to guarantee the geoducks' growth and well-being. These responsibilities include cleaning up any waste or debris that could impede the geoducks' growth, examining the farm for any indications of damage, and ensuring that the substrate is suitable for burrowing.

Additionally, farmers need to keep an eye out for any physical or behavioral anomalies, as well as any indications of illness or stress in the geoducks. To avoid any disruptions, it is imperative to maintain the equipment, making sure that all tools and machinery are in good operating condition.

More involved than routine maintenance, seasonal duties entail getting the farm ready for variations in the weather and surrounding environment.

It is imperative to maintain an ideal water temperature range during the warmer months, and freezing-temperature precautions should be taken during the colder months. To promote the digging activities of the geoducks, seasonal tasks also involve restocking the substrate as needed and modifying feeding regimens to correspond with their growth cycles.

Infrastructure that is meant to resist seasonal storms and tides, including nets and barriers, should also be inspected and maintained.

It's crucial to modify maintenance schedules all year long in response to the shifting requirements of the geoducks and the surrounding circumstances. By being proactive, we can reduce the hazards brought on by harsh weather and other seasonal issues. Frequent regular maintenance improves the farm's overall productivity and sustainability while also ensuring the health and growth of the geoducks.

MONITORING AND CONTROLLING WATER QUALITY

Geoduck cultivation necessitates regular monitoring of water quality because the aquatic environment around them can cause drastic changes that affect the sensitive species. Farmers need to test the water regularly for things like dissolved oxygen levels, pH, salinity, and temperature. For geoducks to remain healthy and grow, certain parameters must be kept within ideal ranges. Frequent monitoring enables the early identification of possible problems that could negatively impact the geoducks, such as pollution, algal blooms, or alterations in the water's chemistry.

To effectively maintain water quality, actions must be taken to correct any deviations from ideal circumstances. For example, farmers may need to use shading or cooling strategies to lower the water temperature if it becomes too high. Aeration systems can be used to promote oxygenation if dissolved oxygen levels fall. Farmers should also set up procedures for handling pollutants, like runoff from adjacent farms or industrial spills, as these can contaminate water supplies with dangerous materials.

Geoducks are supported in having a stable and healthy environment by responsive management techniques and regularly scheduled water quality inspections. These initiatives support the farm's long-term sustainability and productivity in addition to the geoducks' well-being. Farmers can maximize growth rates and lower the danger of sickness and mortality by upholding strict standards for water quality.

CONTROL OF PREDATORS AND INSECTS

Since many marine animals and birds can seriously harm geoducks, controlling predators and pests is an essential part of geoduck farming. Crabs, sea stars, and other fish species are common predators that feed on the young geoducks. Seagulls and other birds may also burrow into the substrate to eat geoducks. Physical barriers that are put in place, such as fences or nets, can successfully ward off these predators.

To find and fix any breaches in these barriers, the farm needs to be regularly patrolled and inspected.

Pests that disturb the substrate and vie for resources, such as burrowing shrimp and specific worm species, can also have an impact on the health of geoducks. These pests can be controlled with the aid of integrated pest management techniques like habitat modification and biological controls. For example, reducing insect populations without using hazardous pesticides can be achieved by changing the substrate composition of the farm or introducing natural predators of the pests.

Effective control of pests and predators depends on timely intervention and continuous observation. A routine for routine inspections should be established, and farmers should keep a record of any activity involving pests or predators. Farmers can safeguard their geoduck populations and maintain a steady and fruitful farming environment by being proactive and employing a mix of physical, biological, and environmental management techniques.

CONTROLLING GEODUCKS' GROWTH AND HEALTH

To maintain ideal development conditions, geoduck growth and health require routine monitoring and treatments. It is important for farmers to regularly weigh and measure geoducks to monitor their growth rates. Any departures from typical growth patterns could be a sign of more serious problems, like poor nutrition or environmental stressors. Ensuring appropriate substrate conditions, modifying feeding schedules and improving water quality are all crucial measures in encouraging healthy growth.

Keeping an eye out for disease or parasite infections is another aspect of health management. Investigating symptoms like lesions, odd behavior, or changes in the look of the shell should be done right away. It is possible to stop the introduction and spread of illnesses by putting biosecurity measures in place, such as clean equipment maintenance and quarantine procedures for new stock.

To reduce losses in situations where the disease is found, speaking with aquatic veterinarians and putting the right therapies into place is essential.

Farmers can make well-informed judgments about farm management strategies by doing routine health checks and keeping thorough records of growth and health data. Farmers can maintain the general health of their geoduck populations by addressing problems early and making necessary adjustments to management tactics. Increased farm productivity, enhanced growth performance, and increased survival rates are all attributed to proactive health management.

MAINTAINING DOCUMENTS AND MANAGING DATA

Succeeding geoduck farming requires efficient data administration and record-keeping. To make well-informed management decisions, it is essential to keep thorough records of all daily operations, water quality assessments, predator and pest incidences, and health checks. By using these records to spot trends and patterns, farmers are better able to foresee possible problems and take action before they become more serious.

To maximize farm operations, data management entails arranging and evaluating the gathered information. Tracking important performance measures like growth rates, survival rates, and yield can be made simpler by using software tools and applications to automate data entry and analysis. Farmers can assess the success of their management strategies and make necessary adjustments to increase production and efficiency by routinely evaluating this data.

Maintaining financial records is crucial for monitoring costs, earnings, and profitability in addition to operational data. Extensive accounting documentation facilitates financial planning and budgeting, guaranteeing the farm's continued viability. In addition to improving daily operations, thorough record-keeping and data management lay the groundwork for long-term strategic planning and ongoing advancements in geoduck farming techniques.

CHAPTER SIX

METHODS OF HARVESTING

CHOOSING THE APPROPRIATE TIME TO HARVEST

It is essential to know when to harvest geoducks to have the best possible production and quality. Geoducks typically attain market scale in around five to seven years. At low tide, when the siphons are more exposed and simpler to find, is usually the optimum time to harvest. Accurate timing can be achieved by keeping an eye on growth rates and environmental factors like water temperature and fertilizer levels.

Before harvesting, make sure the geoducks have attained the appropriate market size through routine sample and size inspections.

It's also critical to pay attention to seasonal fluctuations. Harvesting in the cooler months can be beneficial since it lessens the possibility that the geoducks would experience heat stress, which could lower their quality.

Respecting local laws and ordinances about harvesting seasons is also essential if you want to stay out of trouble and maintain sustainability. These rules frequently seek to preserve the ecology and a robust geoduck population for upcoming farming seasons.

The secret is to schedule and plan well. Farmers commonly use calendars and tracking systems to log the growth and characteristics of their geoduck beds. By using a data-driven strategy, harvesting is done when it's most advantageous, maximizing yield and quality. Farmers can prevent early or delayed harvesting, which can result in financial losses and have an impact on the farm's sustainability, by carefully planning and monitoring their operations.

HARVESTING IMPLEMENTS AND MACHINERY

Proper tool and equipment selection is critical for effective geoduck harvesting. The main instruments are specialty shovels and rakes made to go deeply into the sand without harming the geoducks. To properly penetrate the substrate, these tools frequently include long handles and strong tines. To make it easier to extract the geoducks, high-pressure water jets are also frequently employed to loosen the sand surrounding them.

The harvesters' safety depends on their wearing protective gear. Farmers who operate in damp weather can stay dry and comfortable by donning waterproof suits or waders.

Gloves improve grip on tools and geoducks while shielding hands from abrasions. Mechanized tools like vacuum systems or hydraulic harvesters may be utilized in specific areas to boost productivity, particularly in bigger operations.

After harvest, transport containers are crucial to preserving the quality of the geoducks. To guard against damage and guarantee that the geoducks stay in good condition, these containers need to be strong and have good ventilation. The geoducks can be kept at the ideal temperature with the use of coolers or insulated crates, which lowers the possibility of spoiling while being transported from the harvest location to the processing plant.

METHODICAL HARVESTING PROCEDURE

The first step in the harvesting process is site preparation. This entails putting up the harvest area's boundaries and making sure all required tools and equipment are available. Harvesters begin by excavating the area surrounding the geoduck siphons using rakes or shovels. Digging carefully and thoroughly is essential to prevent harm to the geoducks' bodies. To make extraction easier, high-pressure water jets can be used to remove the surrounding sand.

The geoducks are carefully removed by hand after they become visible. It is important to take care not to break the siphon because doing so could lower its market value. After harvesting, the geoducks are put in transport containers. They should be handled carefully to prevent stress and injury, which can shorten their shelf life and degrade their quality.

To reduce the environmental damage and make the site ready for many agricultural cycles, the extraction site is frequently smoothed over. After that, the geoducks are delivered to a market or processing plant.

It's essential to keep them damp and cool during this time to preserve their quality. When carried out properly, this method guarantees that the geoducks are gathered effectively and responsibly, giving customers high-quality items.

AFTER-HARVEST MANAGEMENT AND PRESERVATION

Handling geoducks after harvest is essential to maintaining their quality and safety. The geoducks should be rinsed with clean, cold water right away after harvesting to get rid of any sand or debris. After that, they ought to be put in vented containers and kept wet with a layer of damp seaweed or something similar. This lessens stress and helps to imitate their natural surroundings.

To avoid spoiling, geoducks should be stored at a low temperature, preferably between 33°F and 40°F. They can be kept in coolers or refrigerated units that maintain a constant temperature. It's crucial to keep them from freezing as doing so could harm their fragile tissues. To keep the geoducks fresh and avoid the accumulation of hazardous gasses, proper ventilation is also essential.

To keep an eye on the geoducks' condition while they are being stored, routine inspections are required. It is important to take quick action in response to any spoiling indicators, such as discoloration or an odd smell.

To avoid infection, the storage room must be kept hygienic and clean. Farmers may guarantee that their geoducks arrive at the market in the best possible shape, ready for consumers to enjoy, by adhering to these post-harvest handling and storage guidelines.

MEASURES OF QUALITY CONTROL

Enforcing strict quality control procedures is necessary to keep geoduck farming up to the high standards required. The first step in ensuring that only geoducks of the right size and condition are chosen is conducting routine checks during the harvesting process. Damaged or undersized geoducks should be thrown away if needed, or put back in the bed to grow larger.

A comprehensive inspection should be carried out after harvest to look for any indications of spoilage, disease, or damage. This includes checking for discoloration, strange smells, and cracks in the shell. It is important to separate any geoducks that don't match quality criteria to avoid contaminating the remaining harvest.

Staff must receive ongoing training on quality control techniques. This guarantees that everyone engaged in the harvesting and handling procedure recognizes the value of upholding high standards and is capable of identifying possible problems. Frequent audits and feedback loops can help to guarantee constant quality throughout the geoduck farming process and enhance procedures. Farmers may guarantee consumer happiness and market success by upholding these quality control procedures, which will preserve the reputation and dependability of their products.

CHAPTER SEVEN

COMPILING AND STOWING

METHODS FOR CLEANING AND PROCESSING

Geoducks must be carefully cleaned and processed to guarantee customer safety and product appeal. To start, give the geoducks a good rinse under cold running water to get rid of any dirt, sand, or other material that might be stuck to their shells. Following the first rinse, the geoduck's siphon undergoes a more thorough cleaning procedure in which the outer skin is meticulously removed. This can be achieved by blanching the geoducks in boiling water for a brief period and then submerging them in ice water. This helps preserve the texture and freshness of the meat and makes peeling the skin easier.

The geoduck can be processed further once the siphon is clean. The meat is meticulously cleaned once the body and shell are separated. This entails making sure that all internal organs are disposed of and extracting any leftover digestive tract components. Depending on the demand in the market, the cleaned meat is subsequently usually chopped into thin strips or left whole. It is essential to keep the work area tidy and hygienic during this process to avoid infection and guarantee that the geoduck meat stays in excellent shape.

Quality control is performed on the geoduck meat following cleaning and processing. To guarantee that only the best parts are packaged for sale, any discolored or broken parts are eliminated. The meat can be packed in ice for short-term storage and transportation, or it can be vacuum-sealed to increase its shelf life and preserve freshness. To maintain the geoducks' quality and safety and prepare them for the market, proper handling and processing methods are crucial.

PACKAGING OPTIONS AND REQUIREMENTS

Proper packaging is crucial for preserving the quality and prolonging the shelf life of geoducks. Vacuum sealing is one of the best techniques since it eliminates air and stops oxidation and bacterial growth.

Geoducks sealed with a vacuum can be kept frozen for extended periods or refrigerated for a few days without experiencing any discernible deterioration in quality. Because it guarantees that the product will stay fresh until it reaches the customer, this strategy is especially well-liked for distribution in the retail and wholesale markets.

Placing the cleaned and processed geoducks in sealed plastic containers is an additional packaging option. To keep the meat fresh, these containers can be packed with ice or filled with a brine solution. Local dissemination and short-term storage are common uses for this technique. Moreover, some processors employ modified atmosphere packaging (MAP), which modifies the packaging's internal atmosphere to delay spoiling and increase shelf life. When sending geoducks to far-off markets, MAP can be very helpful in ensuring that they arrive in ideal condition.

It is essential to choose food-grade materials that do not compromise the safety or taste of the geoduck meat when packing, regardless of the method selected. The date of packaging, storage guidelines, and any other pertinent information should all be prominently shown on labels. In addition to keeping the geoduck flesh safe from contamination and spoiling, proper packaging makes the product look better to customers by guaranteeing they get a premium, fresh item.

ENSURING THE QUALITY AND FRESHNESS OF PRODUCTS

The process of ensuring the quality and freshness of geoduck meat begins as soon as it is harvested. After harvesting, the geoducks must be immediately chilled to prevent bacterial growth and preserve the texture and flavor of the meat. It is recommended that the geoducks be shipped to the processing facility in insulated containers that are packed with ice or cold saltwater. By doing this, the geoduck's natural characteristics are maintained until processing and packaging are possible.

Keeping a cold chain in place throughout processing is essential. While cleaning and packing, the meat should be kept at a temperature that is just above freezing. Maintaining cleanliness and lowering the chance of infection is made easier by using easily cleaned stainless steel tables and equipment. To guarantee that the greatest levels of cleanliness are maintained throughout the processing procedure, workers should wear gloves and hairnets and adhere to stringent hygiene protocols.

The geoduck meat needs to be packaged and kept refrigerated until it's time to ship or sell it. It is important to perform routine quality checks to make sure the meat stays fresh and shows no symptoms of spoiling. Producers may keep an eye on the quality of their product from harvest to the end user by putting in place a strong traceability system. Farmers and processors of Geoduck can guarantee that their products meet consumer expectations and uphold the reputation of their brand by following these guidelines.

CONSIDERATIONS FOR LABELING AND BRANDING

In addition to showcasing the product's distinctive features and giving consumers vital information, labeling and branding are important components of geoduck product marketing. Details like the species name, harvest date, and processing date should all be included on labels that are readable and unambiguous. Cooking directions and nutritional data can also be valuable additions for customers. Information about the farm or area where the geoducks were harvested helps emphasize the product's origin and quality for traceability and consumer confidence.

Branding includes the entire image and perception of the product in addition to the label. A powerful brand can increase customer loyalty and set a producer's geoducks apart from those of rivals. This can be accomplished by using eye-catching package designs, reliable product quality, and captivating marketing strategies that draw attention to the special qualities of geoduck meat, like its flavor, freshness, and use of sustainable farming methods. Using eye-catching photos and logos can improve the product's visual appeal and draw attention when it is displayed on store shelves.

Producers can take part in certification programs that demonstrate their dedication to food safety and sustainability to bolster their branding efforts even more. The product's packaging might prominently feature certifications from reputable organizations to give customers even more confidence about the product's quality and moral standards. Geoduck producers may expand their consumer base and boost their market presence by emphasizing strategic branding and efficient labeling.

GETTING READY FOR MARKET DISTRIBUTION

To guarantee that the product reaches consumers in ideal condition, there are various crucial stages involved in preparing geoducks for market distribution. Making sure that all labeling and packaging are completed accurately and in compliance with regulations is the first step. This entails confirming that the labels are correct, the containers are appropriately packed, and all pertinent information is there. Once geoducks have been correctly packaged and labeled, they are kept in refrigerators to preserve their freshness until they are ready to be shipped.

Planning your logistics is essential for effective market distribution. Farmers who grow geoduck must work with retailers and distributors to decide on the most efficient ways to ship their goods. To keep the cold chain intact during transit, this frequently entails the use of refrigerated vehicles or containers. Air freight could be required for international shipments to guarantee that the geoducks arrive at their destination promptly and in top shape. This process can be made more efficient and the chance of delays or spoiling decreased by working with a trustworthy logistics partner.

It also takes a solid grasp of consumer tastes and market demand to distribute products effectively. Retailers and wholesalers should collaborate closely with producers to estimate demand and modify production schedules accordingly. This guarantees that there is always an adequate supply of fresh geoducks and helps avoid overproduction.

CHAPTER EIGHT

STRATEGIES FOR MARKETING AND SALES

FINDING THE RIGHT TARGET MARKETS

Having a clear understanding of your target market is essential to running a profitable farming enterprise. Commence by investigating the age range, financial status, and geographic location of possible clients. For example, because geoduck is considered a delicacy, high-end eateries and seafood shops in urban regions are probably regular clients. Cultural preferences also matter a lot; areas with a long history of seafood consumption, especially in East Asia, can be very lucrative markets.

Think about the various subgroups that fall under these more general categories to further narrow down your target audience. Different market sectors include affluent people looking for fine dining experiences, consumers who are health-conscious and curious about the nutritional value of geoduck, and foodies who like making novel recipes at home. You may more successfully adapt your marketing techniques to these groups' expectations by being aware of their unique demands and preferences.

Participating in focus groups, questionnaires, and internet forums with prospective clients can yield insightful information about their preferences and purchasing habits. Using this data can help you develop product offerings and advertising strategies that are specifically targeted to your target market. Selecting the appropriate target market increases consumer satisfaction and loyalty in addition to increasing marketing efficiency.

FORMULATING A MARKETING STRATEGY

Your geoduck farming business will not succeed until you create a thorough marketing plan. Start by establishing specific, attainable goals that complement your overarching business goals. These objectives can be expanding into new markets, raising revenues, or raising brand awareness.

After your objectives have been determined, list the precise plans and methods you'll employ to reach them. A combination of direct sales, public relations, and internet marketing may be used for this.

Your plan should be built around digital marketing. Employ email marketing, social media platforms, and search engine optimization (SEO) to reach a large audience. Social media sites like Facebook and Instagram work wonders for displaying your product through eye-catching images and videos of the geoduck farming process and its culinary applications. Investing in an e-commerce website that is easy to use can also draw in online customers and make direct transactions easier.

Public relations is another essential element of your marketing strategy. Developing connections with media outlets, chefs, and food bloggers can result in beneficial PR. Organizing activities like cooking demos or farm tours can draw interest in and generate talk about your goods.

Through the integration of various initiatives with unified branding and messaging, you can efficiently advertise your geoduck merchandise and increase revenue.

ESTABLISHING A NAME AND CREDIBILITY

To stand out in a crowded market, you must build a solid brand and reputation for your geoduck farming operation. Establish your brand identity at the outset by outlining your values, mission, and USPs. Every element of your company, from your packaging and logo to your customer service and marketing materials, should represent this brand. Consumer awareness and trust are increased when a brand is authentic and well-coordinated.

Subsequently, concentrate on providing superior items and outstanding customer support. Ensuring consistency in product quality is essential to preserving consumer happiness and loyalty. To make sure your geoducks live up to client expectations and industry standards, put in place strict quality control procedures.

Additionally, you may improve your reputation and promote repeat business by offering exceptional customer service, which includes prompt responses to requests and individualized interactions.

Building relationships with stakeholders and the community is another powerful strategy for enhancing your reputation and brand. Engage in community activities, provide your support to environmental sustainability projects, and be open about your farming methods. Establishing your company as a socially conscious and community-minded organization will help you spread goodwill and favorable word-of-mouth, which will increase the visibility of your brand in the marketplace.

DIRECT, WHOLESALE, AND INTERNET SALES CHANNELS

To increase your geoduck farming business's reach and profitability, you must diversify your sales channels. Selling directly to consumers, such as at farmers' markets or from your storefront, enables you to engage with them one-on-one and develop relationships. This strategy builds a devoted client base and offers quick feedback. Furthermore, arranging sampling events or providing farm tours might improve the direct sales process and draw in additional customers.

Distribution through wholesalers is another important sales route. You can expand your market reach considerably by forming partnerships with specialty grocery stores, upscale dining establishments, and seafood distributors.

Building trust and showcasing the constant caliber of your goods is essential to forming these alliances. Reaching out to potential wholesale buyers can be accomplished through networking within the business, participating in food expos, and offering samples.

A practical and scalable approach to reach a larger audience is through online sales. Regardless matter where they are in the world, clients can buy geoducks straight from you by creating an online store. To draw in organic visitors, make sure your website is search engine optimized and user-friendly. You can also reach a wider audience by using seafood-specific platforms or internet marketplaces like Amazon. Providing adaptable delivery choices and making sure freshness is properly packaged are essential for preserving consumer happiness in online purchases.

RELATIONSHIP MANAGEMENT AND CUSTOMER SERVICE

To establish long-lasting relationships and guarantee the success of your geoduck farming business, you must deliver exceptional customer service. First, ensure that your employees are attentive to consumer inquiries and have a thorough understanding of your items. Timely and polite communication facilitates speedy problem-solving and creates a good first impression. To monitor interactions and customize your service, think about putting in place a customer relationship management (CRM) system.

Proactive customer care goes beyond meeting urgent requirements and can increase loyalty.

After a customer makes a purchase, follow up with them to get their opinion and show your appreciation. Maintaining constant contact with them through newsletters or customized offers makes your brand memorable and promotes recurring business. Social networking may be a useful tool for communicating with clients, responding to inquiries, and providing information on your farm and merchandise.

Strong relationships are cultivated via more than just business dealings. Share tales about your farming methods, environmental initiatives, and community service to connect with your customers. Organizing events like culinary lessons or farm tours enables consumers to engage with your business more deeply. Building a community and showing real concern for your clients will help you create a devoted following of customers who will support your business in the long run and act as brand ambassadors.

CHAPTER NINE

PLANNING AND FINANCIAL MANAGEMENT

FINANCIAL PLANNING AND BUDGETING

Financial planning and budgeting are essential for success when starting a geoduck farm. Start by listing every possible expense, such as the cost of labor, seedlings, land preparation, equipment purchase, and continuing upkeep. To get an exact assessment of these costs, do an extensive study. In addition, provide for unanticipated costs by setting aside money in a contingency fund to reduce risks.

Next, make a thorough budget that breaks down costs into manageable categories and allocates actual costs to each one.

Revenue estimates based on geoduck market pricing and expected harvest yields should also be included in this budget. To stay on course and adjust to shifting market conditions or unforeseen expenses, evaluate and tweak your budget regularly.

Beyond creating a budget, financial planning also entails managing debt, cash flow, and investment choices. To create a thorough financial strategy customized to the particular requirements and objectives of your geoduck farming endeavor, think about speaking with a financial advisor with experience in the agricultural industry.

SOURCES OF FUNDING AND GRANTS

A geoduck farming operation must first secure money to get off the ground and remain operational. Investigate your options for finance, such as government subsidies for agricultural projects, bank or credit union loans for agriculture, and private investors willing to fund sustainable aquaculture initiatives.

Grants and subsidies are frequently provided by municipal, state, and federal governments, especially for agricultural projects. Since the application process for these grants may be competitive and time-consuming, do your research and apply as soon as possible.

Furthermore, take into account agreements with conservation organizations that support ecologically friendly farming techniques or crowd funding sites.

To recruit financial partners, create a convincing business strategy that highlights the potential profitability, environmental sustainability, and community impact of your geoduck farming operation. Work together with industry associations or agricultural extension agencies to get advice on how to find funding sources and submit grant applications successfully.

ANALYZING PROFITABILITY AND CONTROLLING COSTS

In geoduck farming, cost control strategies that work are critical to maximizing revenue. Regularly track and evaluate production costs to find areas where costs can be cut without sacrificing output or quality. Reduce input costs by putting into practice effective agricultural techniques like careful seedling selection, tailored feeding schedules, and strategic site management.

Perform a comprehensive profitability analysis by contrasting the revenue from geoduck sales with the costs of production and overhead. To evaluate the profitability of your farm and find areas for increasing operational effectiveness and optimizing returns on investment, use financial ratios and performance measures.

To assess the viability of new technologies, equipment upgrades, or production expansions, do ongoing cost-benefit analyses. To obtain insights into the best strategies for cost reduction and profitability enhancement in the aquaculture sector, consult with industry professionals or other geoduck producers.

MAINTAINING FINANCIAL RECORDS

Tracking costs, earnings, and overall financial performance in geoduck farming requires precise and well-organized record-keeping. Establish a reliable accounting system that frequently produces financial reports, keeps thorough records of income and expenses, and classifies transactions.

To ensure that tax laws and reporting requirements are followed, use certified accountants with knowledge in agriculture finance or use accounting software to automate record-keeping procedures. Maintain complete records of all financial transactions, contracts, receipts, and invoices about your geoduck farming business.

To ensure financial responsibility and transparency, keep an eye on cash flow, inventory levels, and bank statement reconciliation regularly. To avoid mistakes, fraud, or inconsistencies in your farm's financial records and operations, set up internal controls and procedures for financial management.

GETTING READY FOR AUDITS AND TAXES

Being compliant and having a successful geoduck farming business requires careful preparation for taxes. Learn about the tax laws and rules that apply to agricultural businesses, such as property taxes, sales taxes, income taxes, and any special tax breaks or incentives that may be offered to aquaculture businesses.

To ensure correct tax reporting and filing, keep thorough records of your income, expenses, assets, and liabilities. To maximize tax strategies, reduce tax liabilities, and guarantee timely filing of tax returns and payments, confer with tax experts or accountants who specialize in agricultural taxation.

Maintaining well-organized financial records, supporting documentation, and audit trails for each financial transaction will help you get ready for any future audits. Regularly carry out internal audits to find and address any inconsistencies or compliance problems early on. Work together with legal or professional advisors to minimize risks related to tax-related assessments or inquiries, and to successfully manage tax audits.

CHAPTER TEN

FAQS & FREQUENTLY ASKED QUESTIONS

TROUBLESHOOTING TYPICAL PROBLEMS

There will inevitably be difficulties while getting started in the geoduck farming industry. Water quality is a common problem that farmers may encounter. Stress brought on by low water quality can have an impact on geoducks' growth and general health. Regular water testing is essential to ensure ideal conditions for your geoducks and to help resolve this. Any problems with water quality can be lessened by adjusting the pH, temperature, and oxygen content of the water as necessary.

Predator control is yet another prevalent worry. Predators including sea otters, crabs, and some fish species can harm geoducks. Protecting your geoduck beds can be achieved by putting in place physical barriers or netting to dissuade predators. Predators can have a major negative influence on your farm, but they can be minimized with routine monitoring and prompt action against possible threats.

Furthermore, controlling illness is a crucial component of geoduck farming. If diseases like Red Tide or bacterial infections are not treated quickly, geoduck populations can be destroyed.

The long-term health of your geoducks can be ensured by creating a thorough disease management strategy that includes routine health checks, quarantine protocols for sick individuals, and professional collaboration. This will help minimize disease outbreaks.

FAQS REGARDING FARMING METHODS ON GEODUCK

If you're new to geoduck farming, you probably have a few questions about optimal practices. A frequently asked question relates to seed selection. To ensure a successful farming endeavor, it is imperative to select healthy and genetically diverse geoduck seeds from reliable sources. For seeds to survive and flourish, proper handling and acclimatization to farm conditions are also essential.

Concerning nutrition and feeding, this is another commonly asked subject. Filter feeders and geoducks mostly eat phytoplankton and other minute aquatic creatures. Recognizing the dietary requirements of geoducks and offering more feed when required will help them grow more quickly and provide larger harvests. Important procedures in geoduck farming include tracking feeding patterns and modifying feed amounts in response to environmental changes.

Moreover, farmers frequently have questions regarding harvesting methods. Excavation must be done carefully when harvesting geoducks to protect the surrounding ecology and the shells. Harvesting can go more smoothly and effectively if specific tools are used and established standards are followed. Harvested geoducks must be handled and transported properly to preserve their quality until they are sold.

MANAGING ENVIRONMENTAL DIFFICULTIES

Numerous environmental elements that can affect agricultural productivity are influenced by geoduck farming. Variations in water temperature are a major challenge. Because geoducks like steady water temperatures, it can be beneficial to reduce temperature fluctuations by using thermal control systems, water movement, or shading.

Silt accumulation and sedimentation in geoduck beds are further environmental concerns. Geoduck growth and eating can be hampered by excessive sedimentation that buries them. The health of geoduck populations can be maintained by implementing sediment control methods like silt curtains, routine dredging, or changing farming practices to prevent sedimentation.

Climate change and ocean acidification are further long-term obstacles to geoduck farming. Reducing carbon emissions, implementing sustainable practices, and keeping an eye on water chemistry can all help to lessen the impact of environmental changes on geoduck habitats. Farmers can adjust to changing environmental conditions by working with environmental specialists and remaining up to date on current research.

ANSWERING REGULATORY INQUIRIES

Successful geoduck farming enterprises depend on successfully navigating the regulatory environment. A frequently asked regulatory query relates to licenses and permissions. The first steps in establishing a geoduck farm are obtaining the required permits from local authorities and adhering to rules for water use, environmental impact assessments, and species protection.

Standards for food safety and quality are another area of regulation. Farmers of geoducks are required to follow food safety regulations, which include processing, storing, and appropriately transporting harvested geoducks. By putting in place traceability procedures, hygienic procedures, and routine contamination testing, geoducks can be made to satisfy consumer demands and industry standards.

Farmers also frequently ask about land use and zoning laws. Selecting a site and growing a farm require knowledge of zoning regulations about protected areas, coastal development, and aquaculture. Farmers can efficiently handle compliance obligations by working with regulatory bodies, getting legal guidance, and being informed about changes to the law.

EXTENDED SUSTAINABILITY MEASURES

To protect resources and maintain the industry's profitability for future generations, geoduck farming must be sustainable. The preservation of habitat is a crucial aspect of sustainability. Maintaining ecological balance involves limiting habitat disturbance during farming operations, recovering damaged areas, and protecting native geoduck habitats.

The efficient use of resources is a further sustainability priority. Geoduck farms can lessen their environmental impact by implementing water conservation techniques, improving energy consumption, and lowering waste generation.

Sustainable resource management is facilitated by the adoption of cutting-edge technologies like renewable energy sources and recirculating aquaculture systems.

In addition, long-term sustainability depends on fostering biodiversity and ecosystem resilience. Marine ecosystems Eare maintained when native species variety is encouraged, pollution inputs are kept to a minimum, and conservation efforts are undertaken. A more resilient and ecologically conscious geoduck farming sector can be promoted by interacting with stakeholders, exchanging best practices, and supporting sustainable aquaculture laws.

www.ingramcontent.com/pod-product-compliance
Lightning Source LLC
Chambersburg PA
CBHW071838210526
45479CB00001B/185